Unicorn Coloring Book

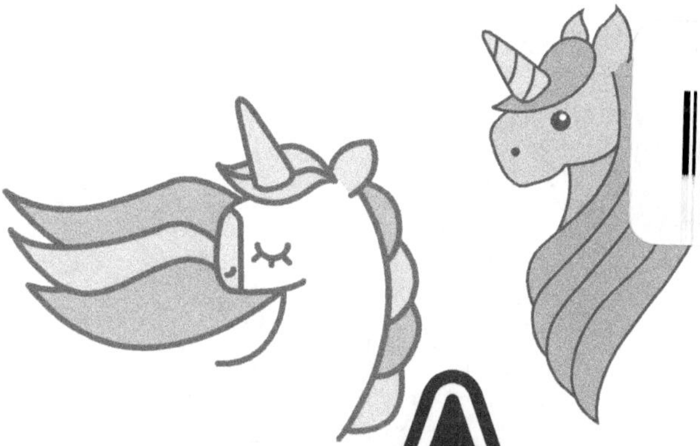

This book belongs to:

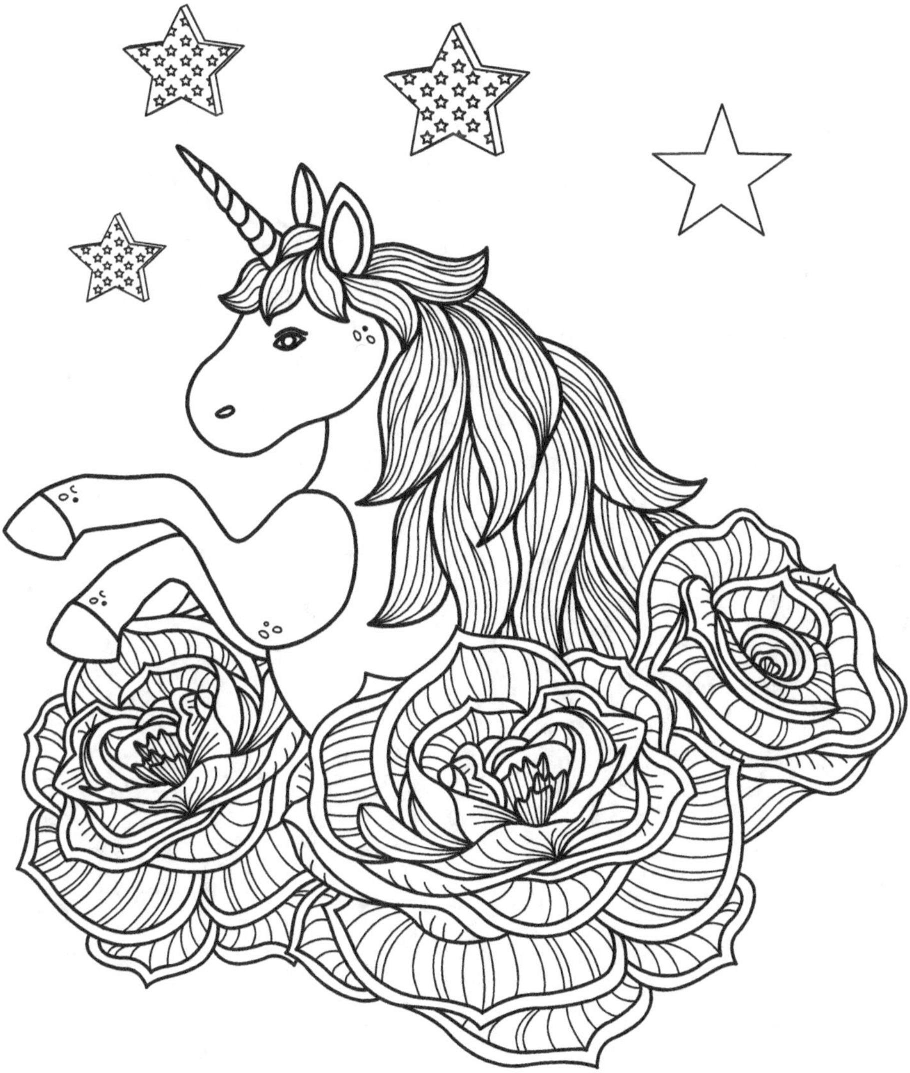

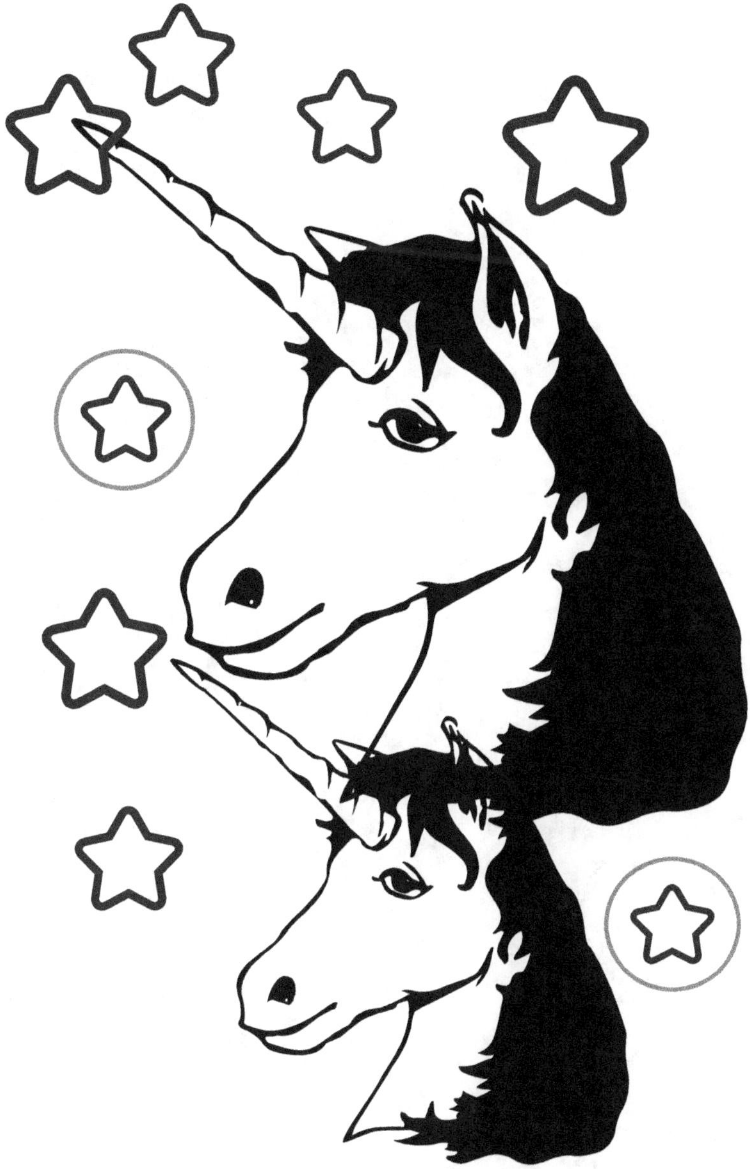

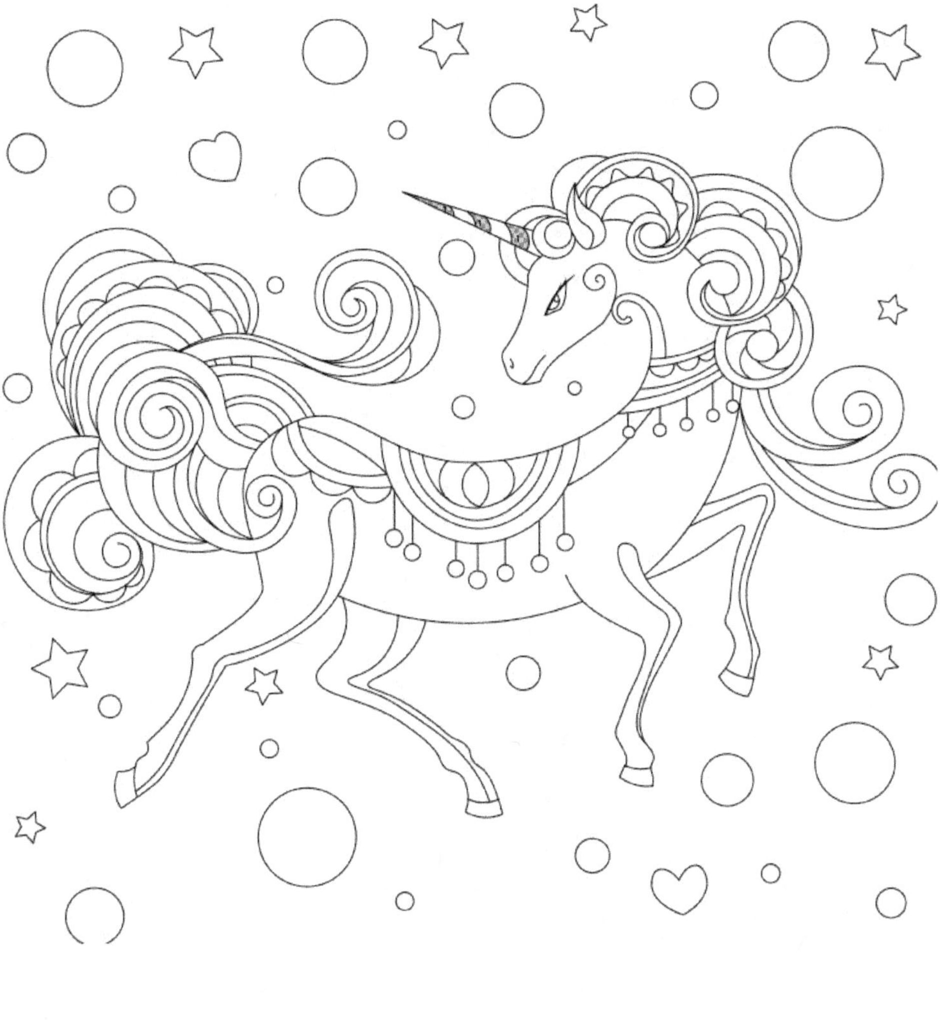

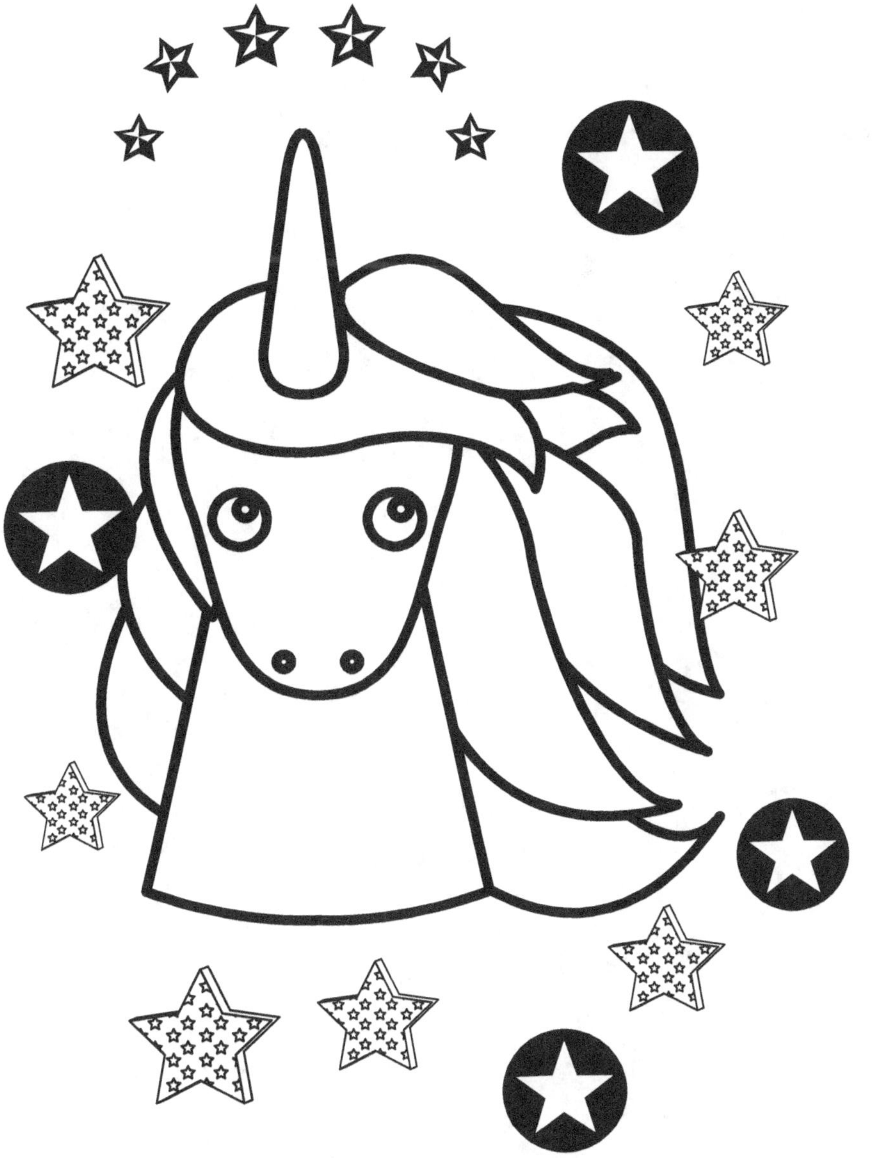

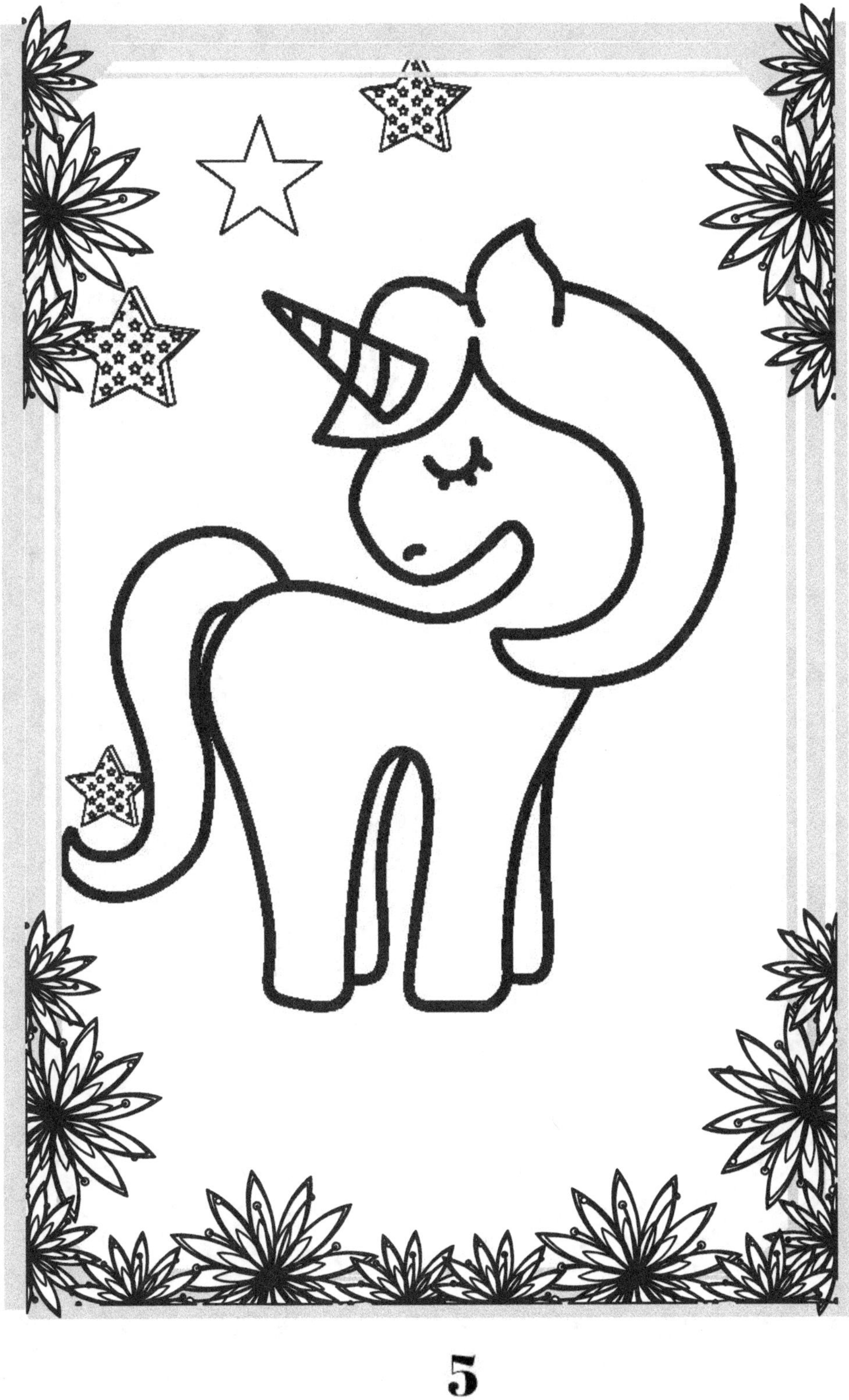

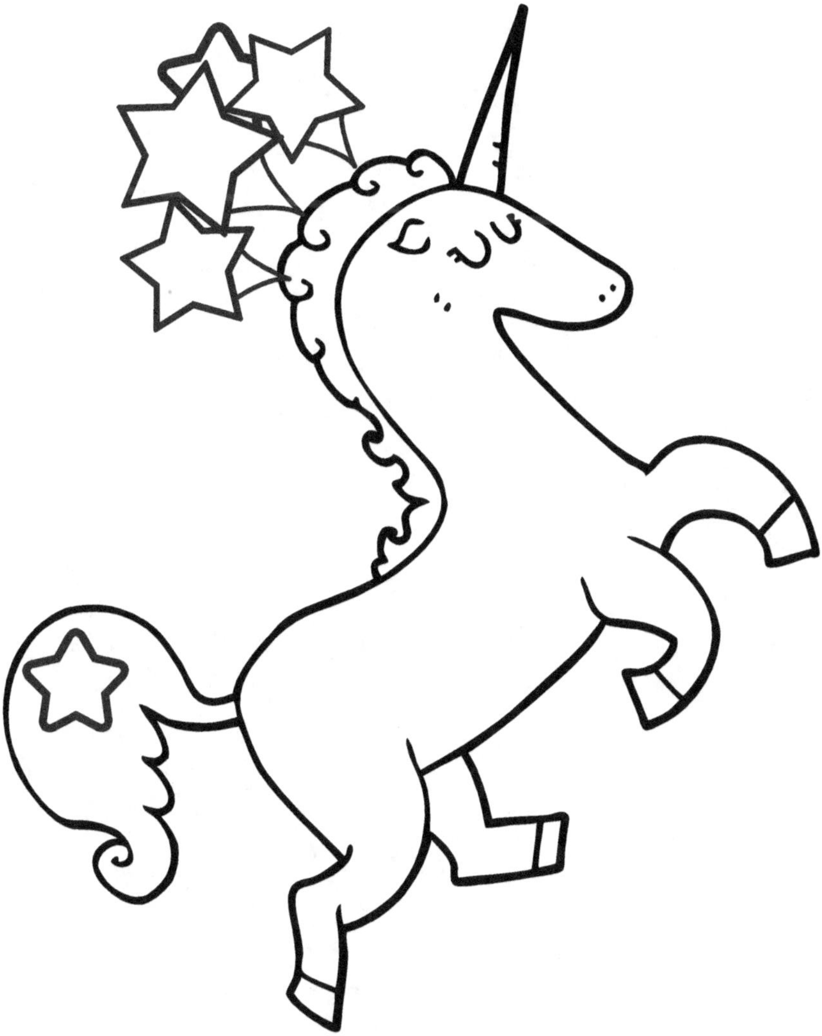

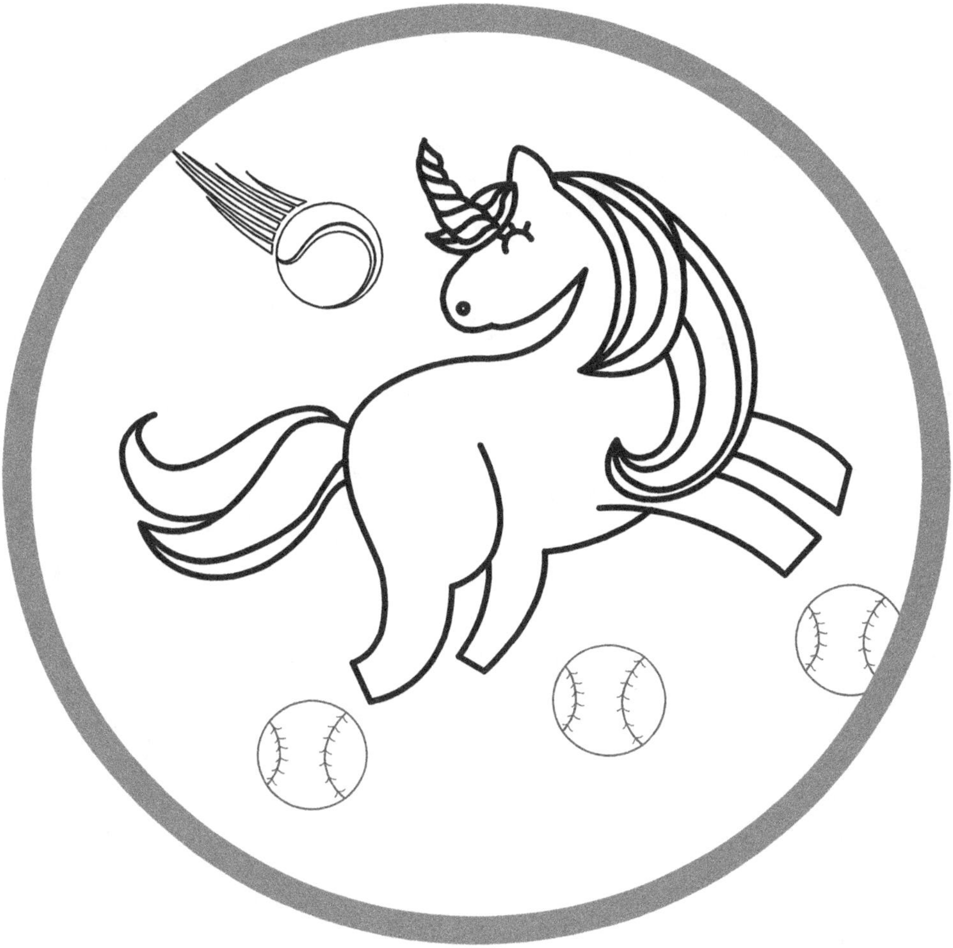

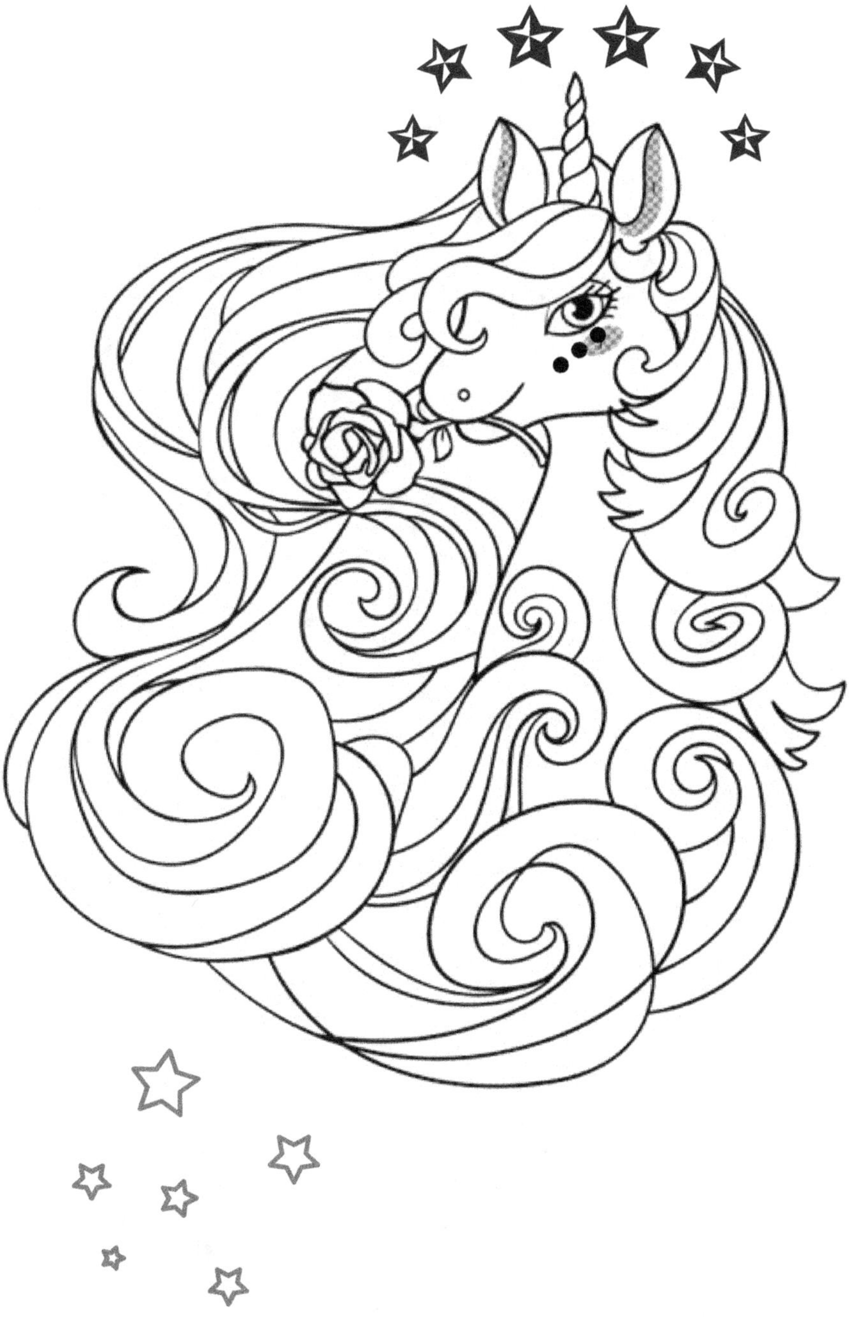

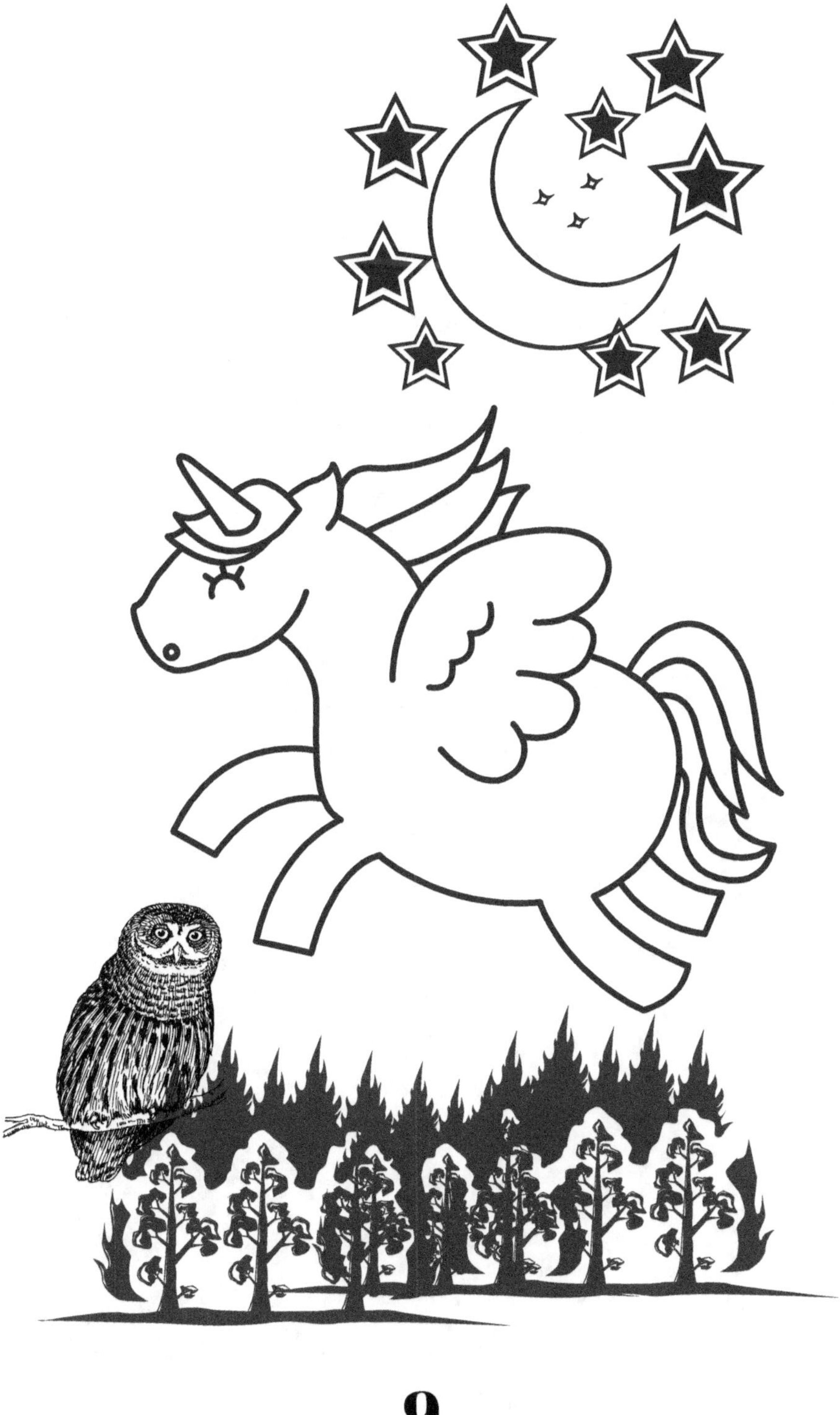

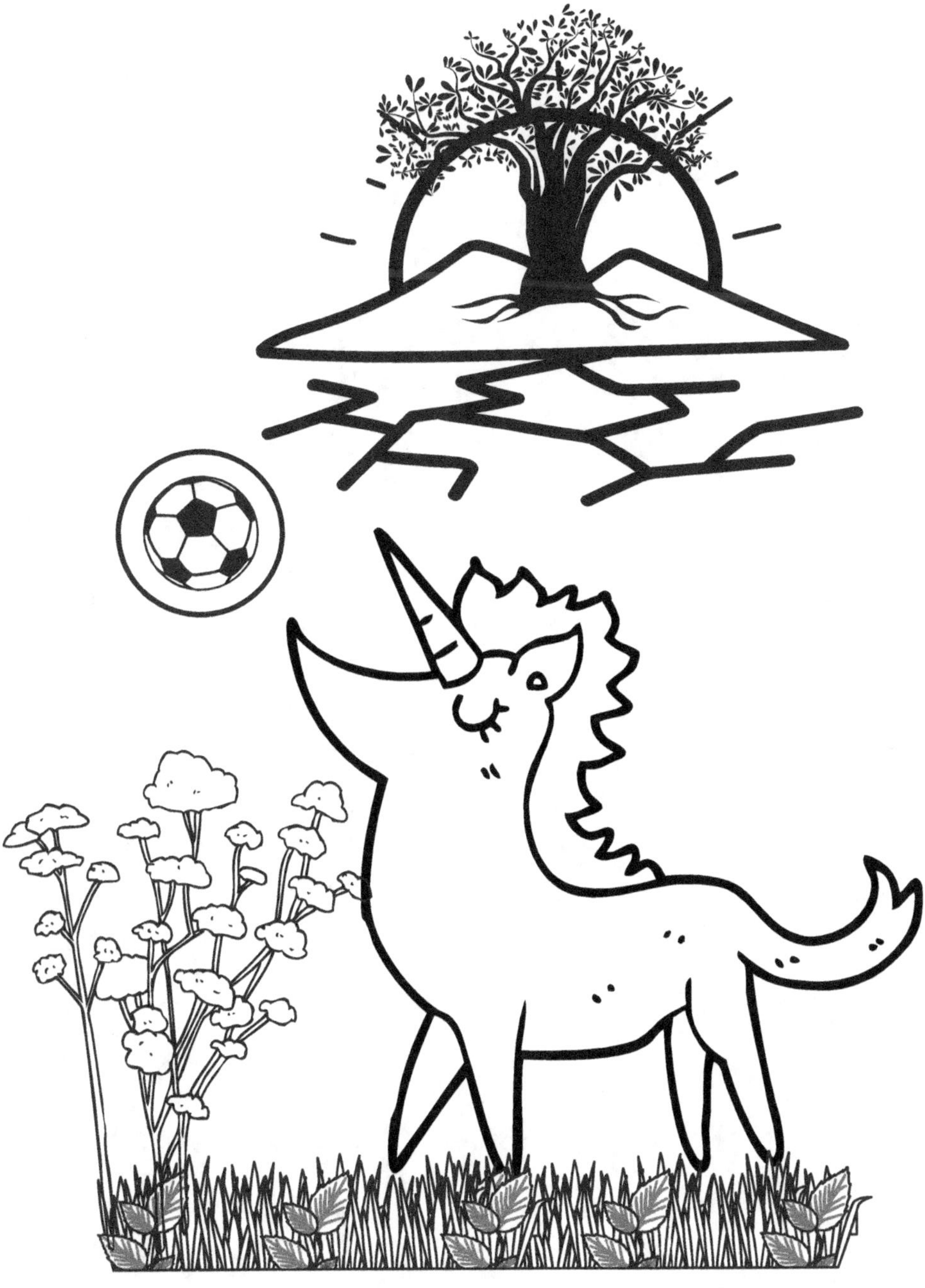

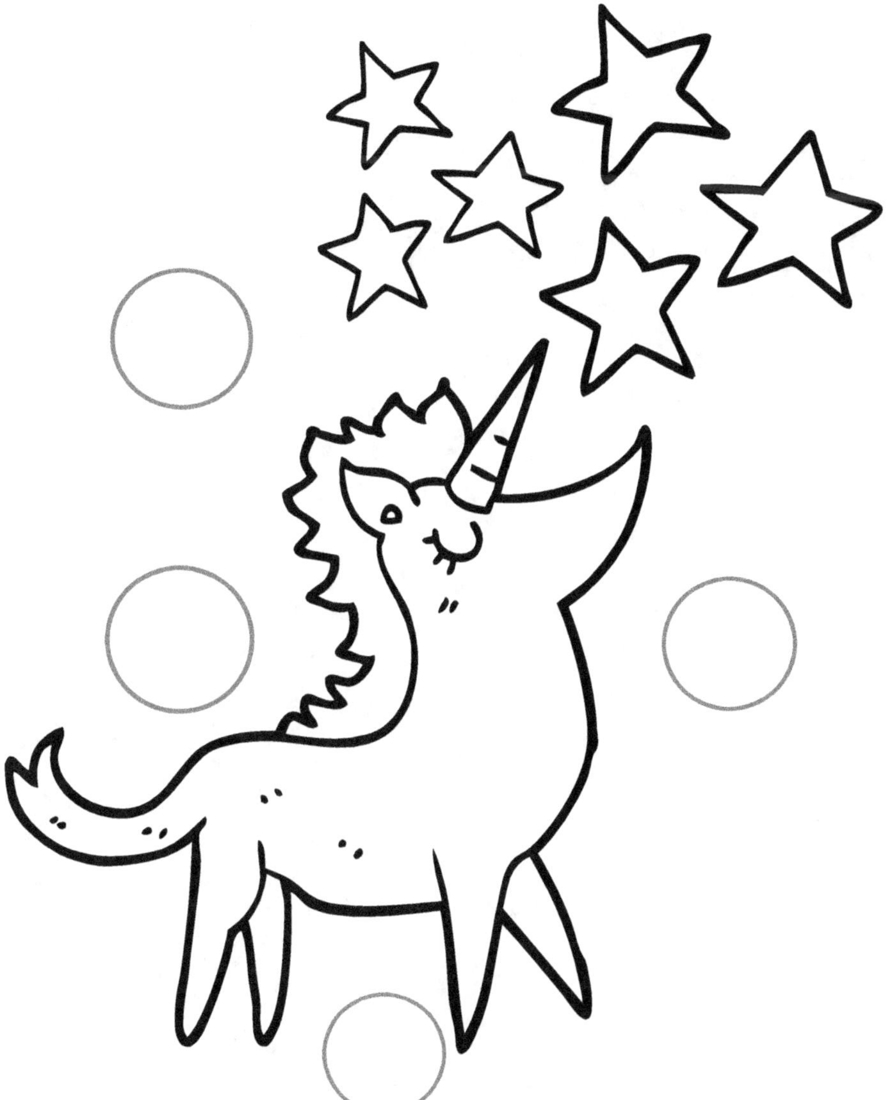

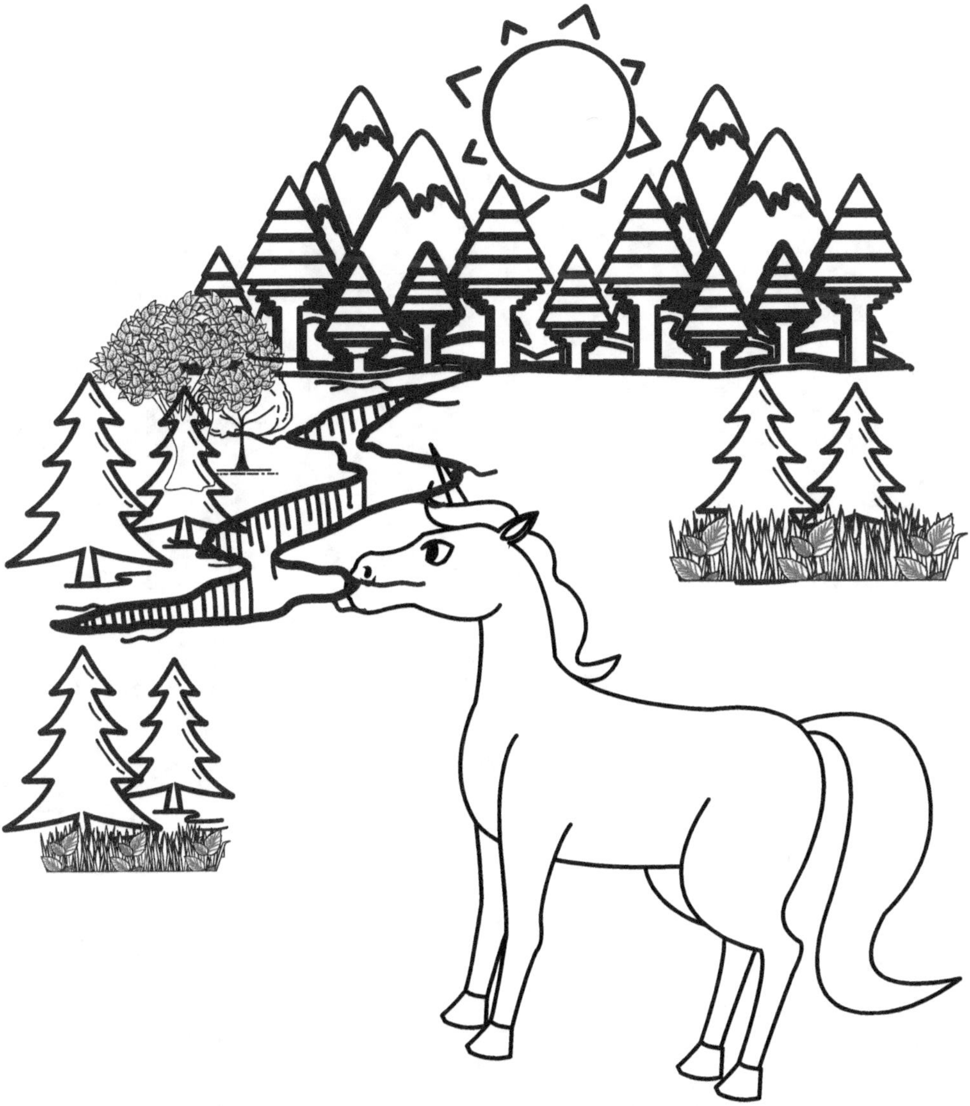

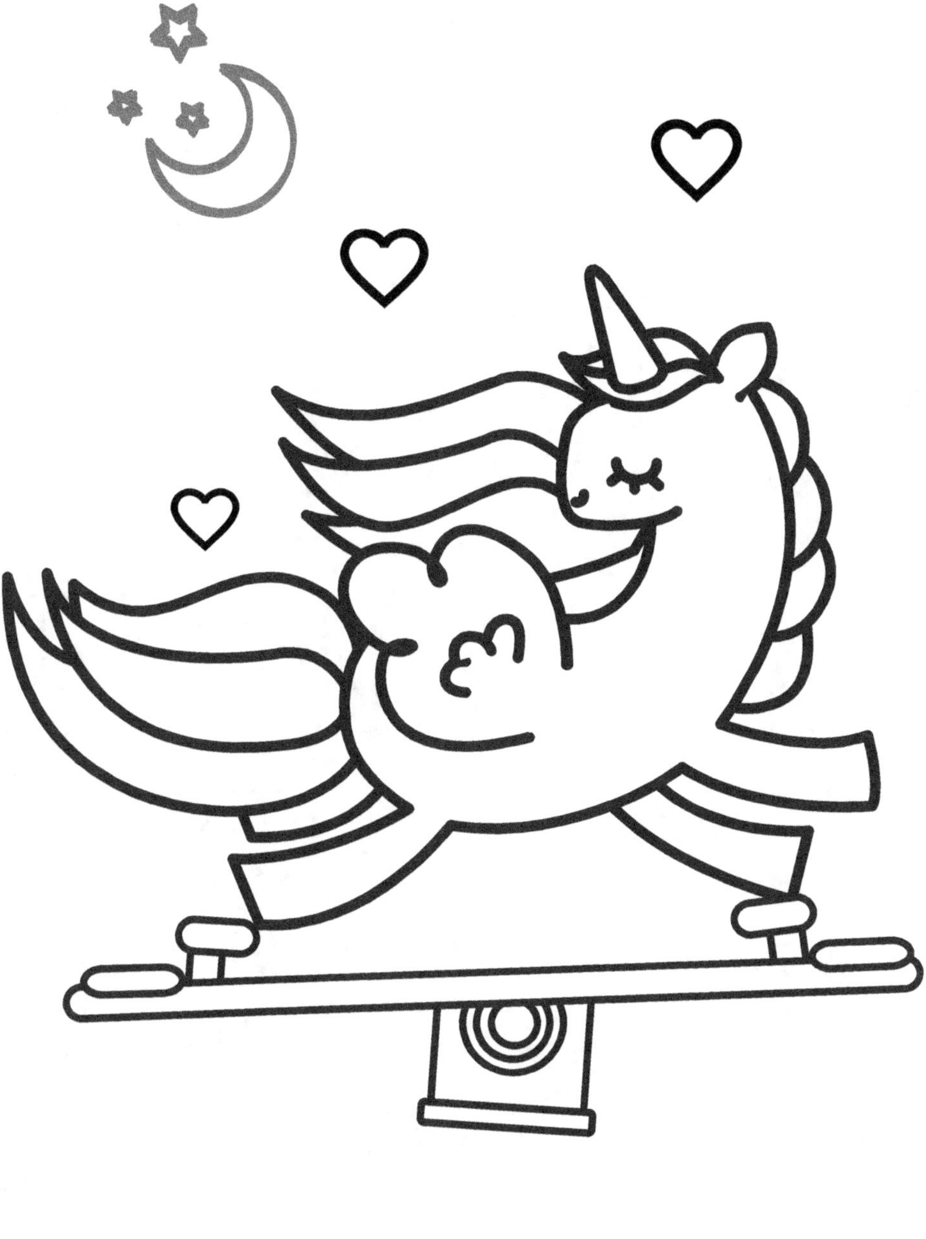

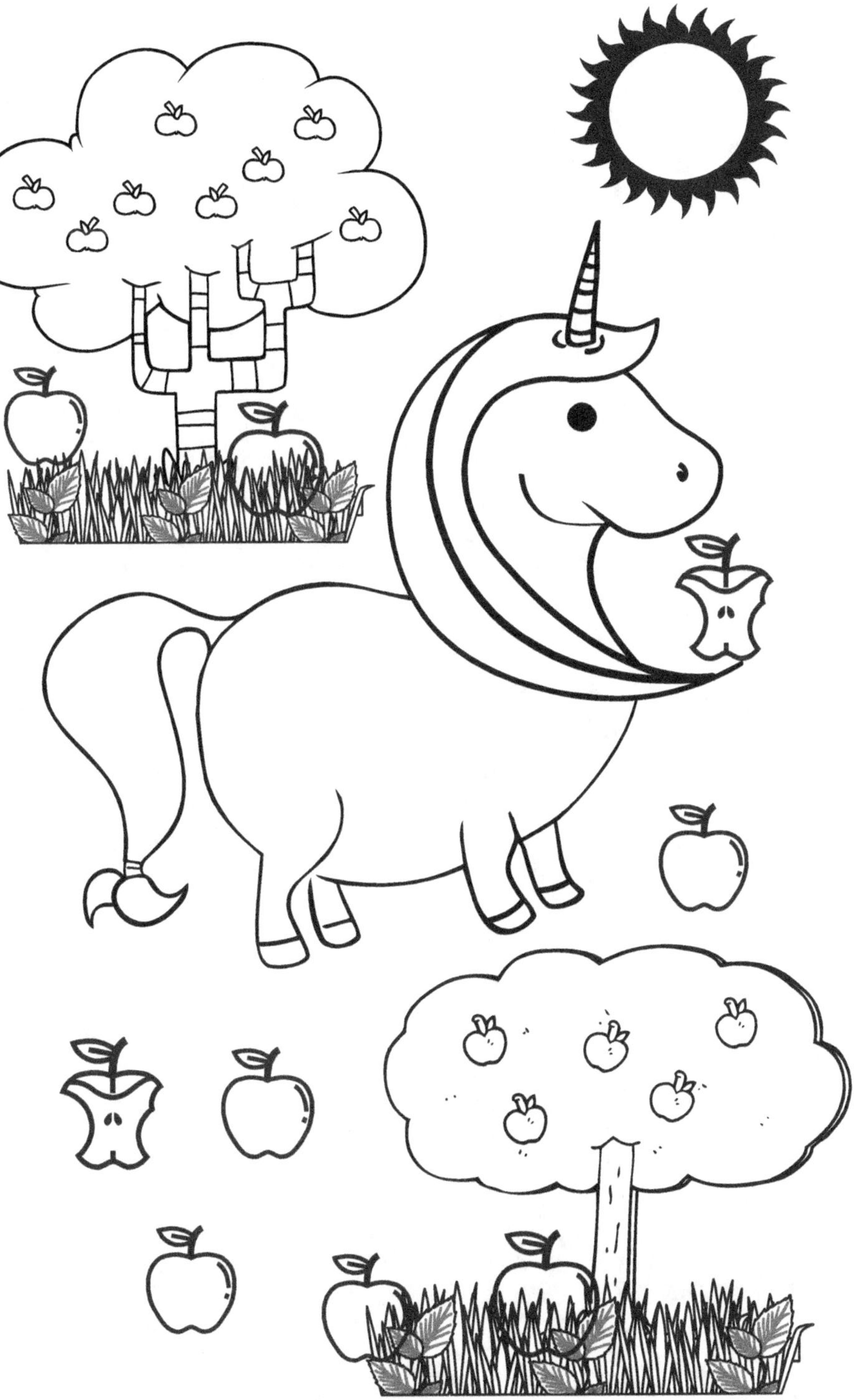

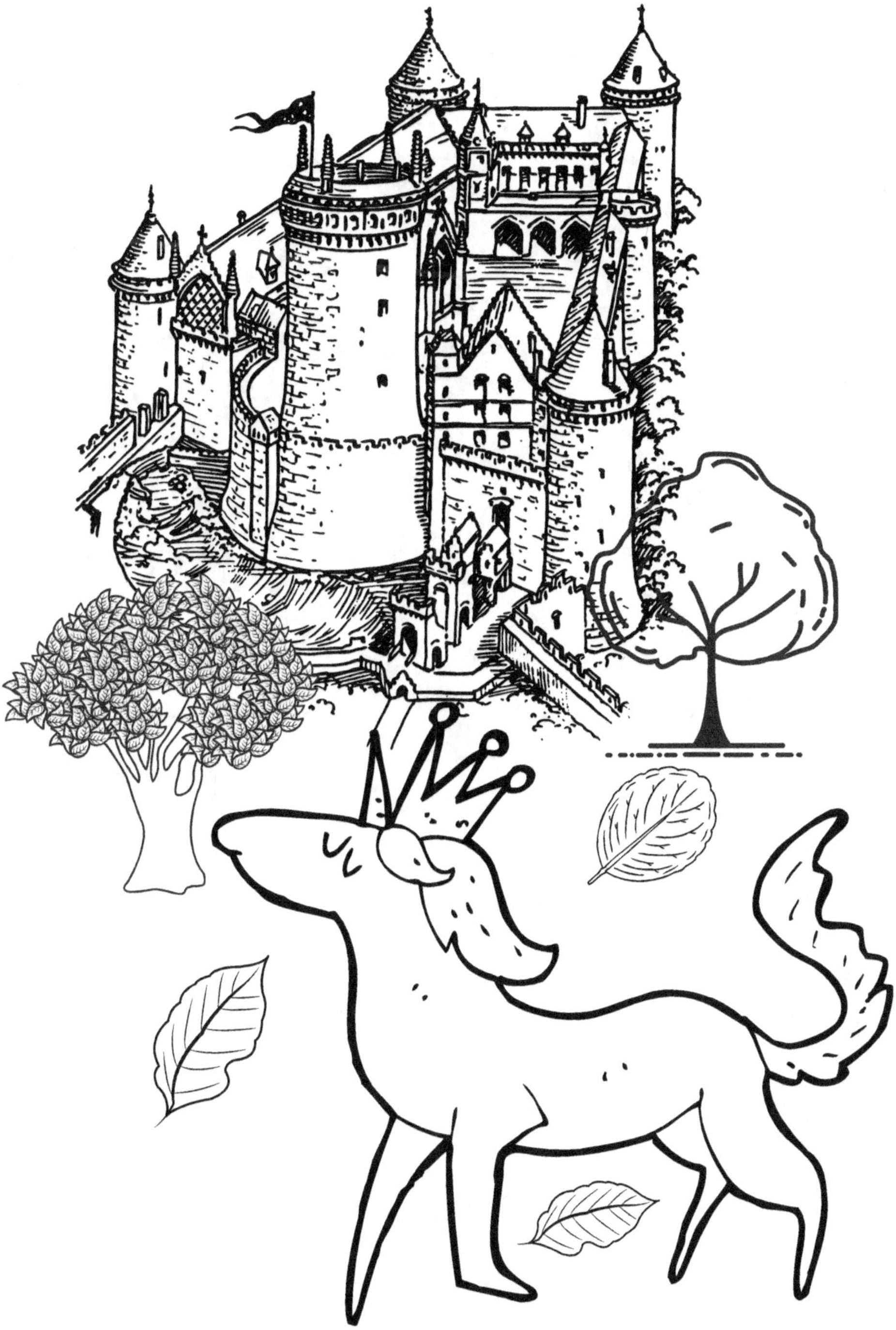

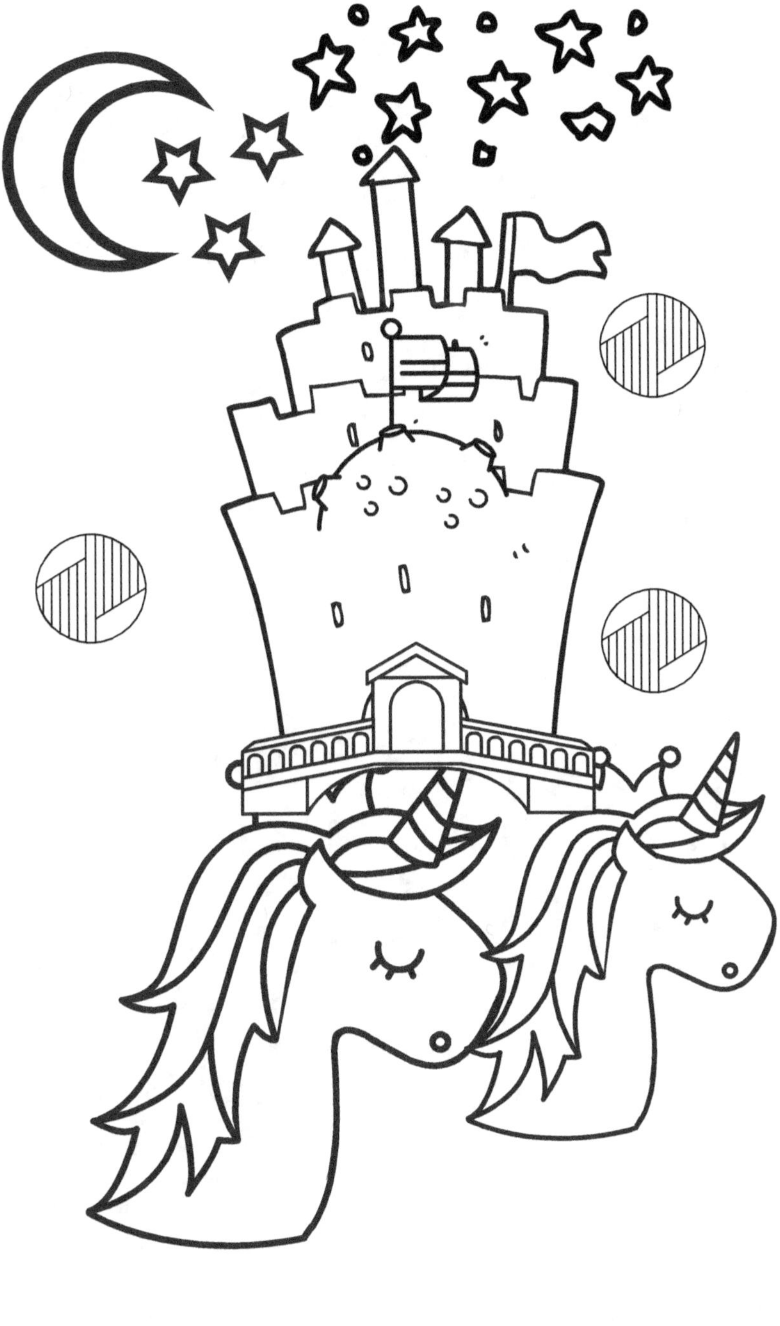

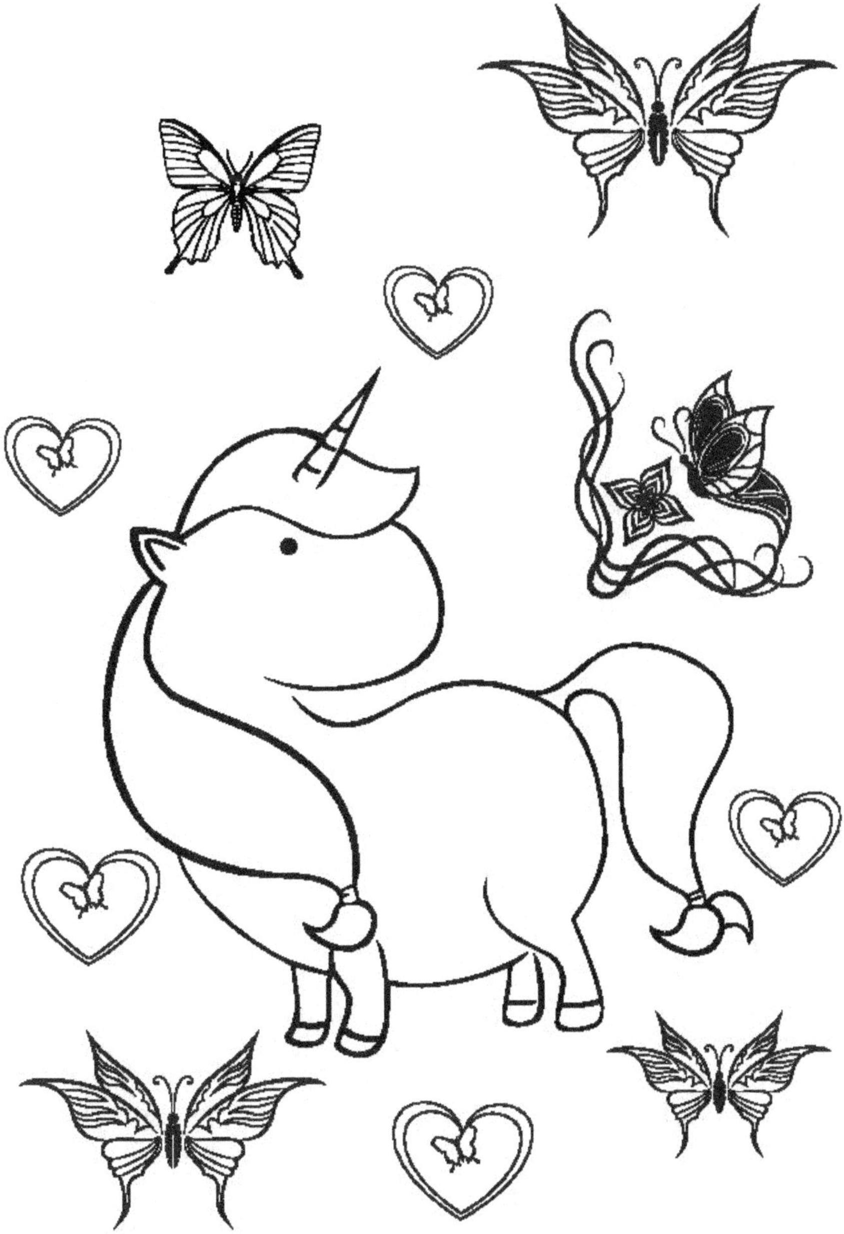

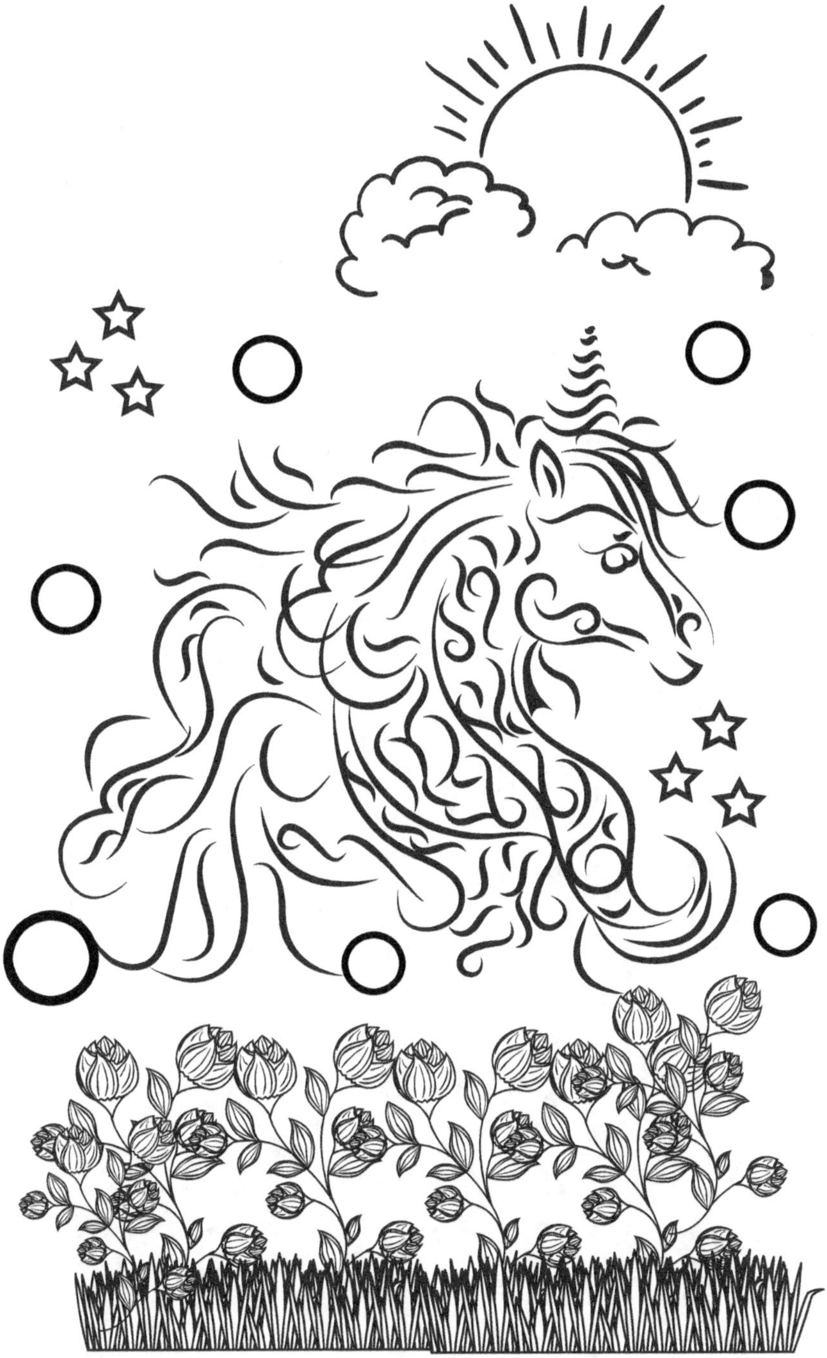

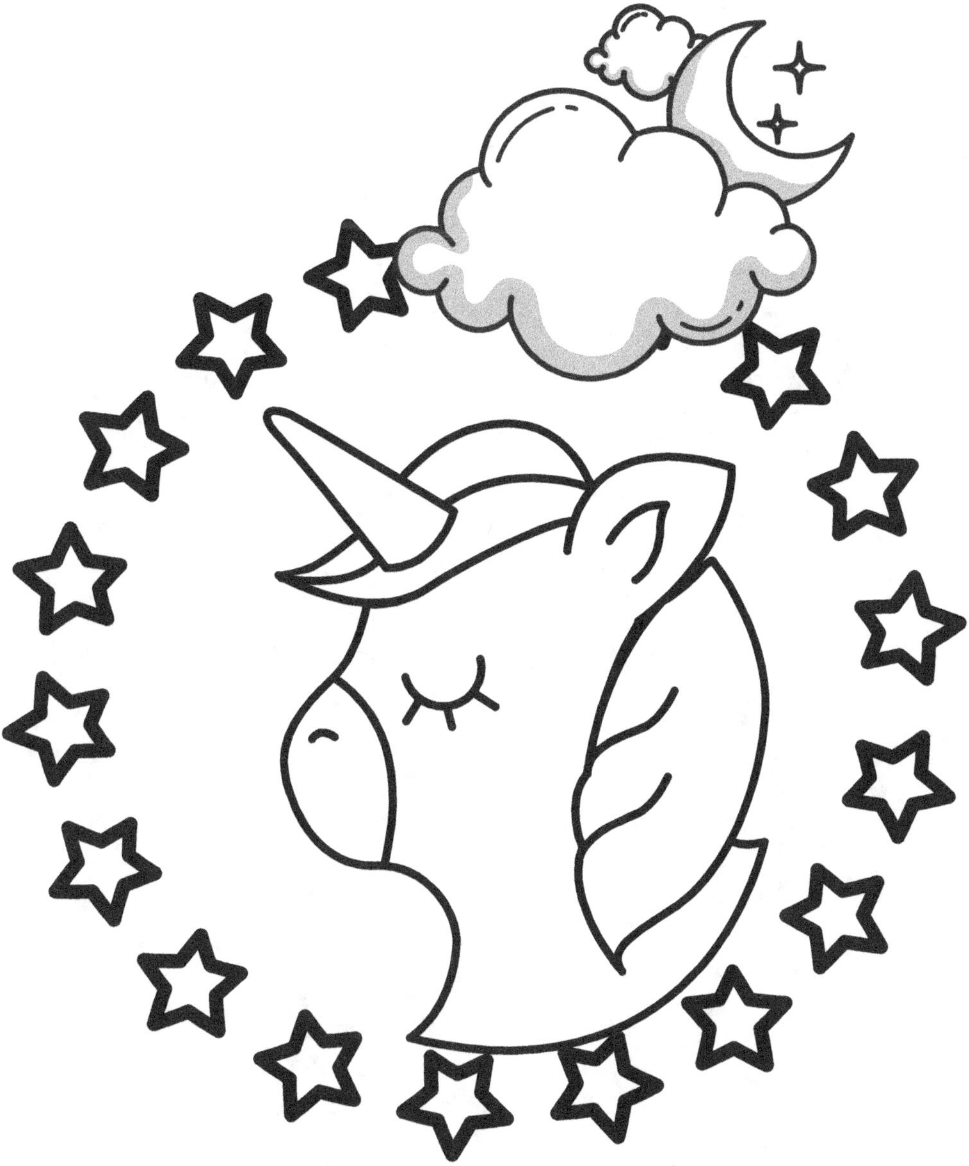

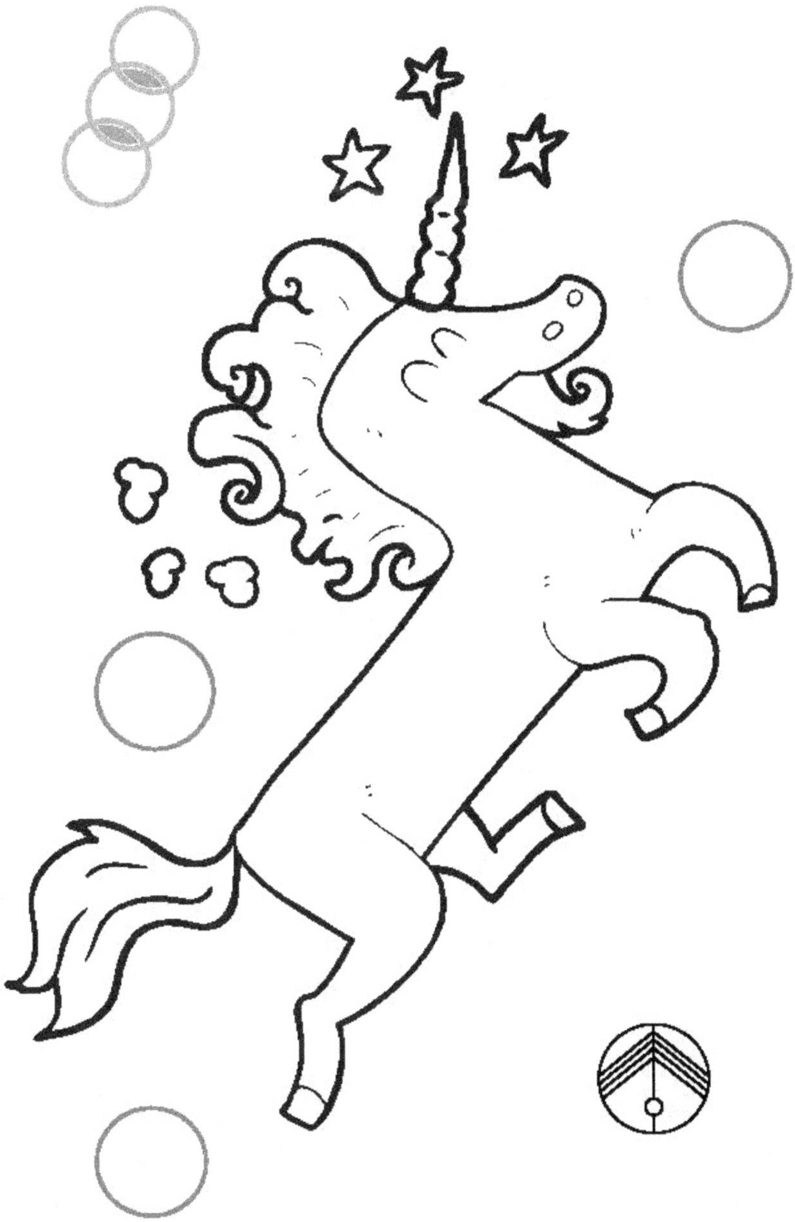

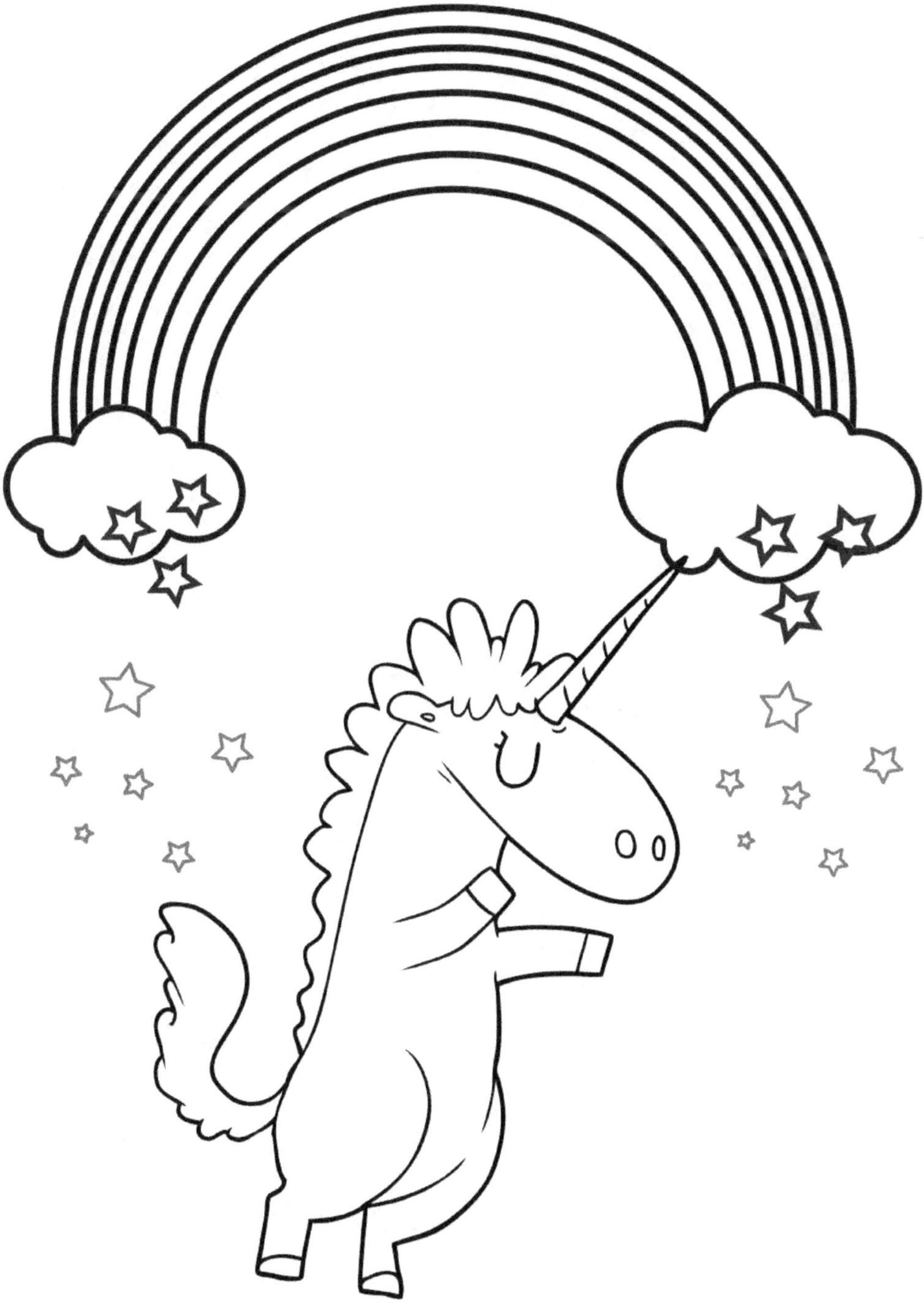

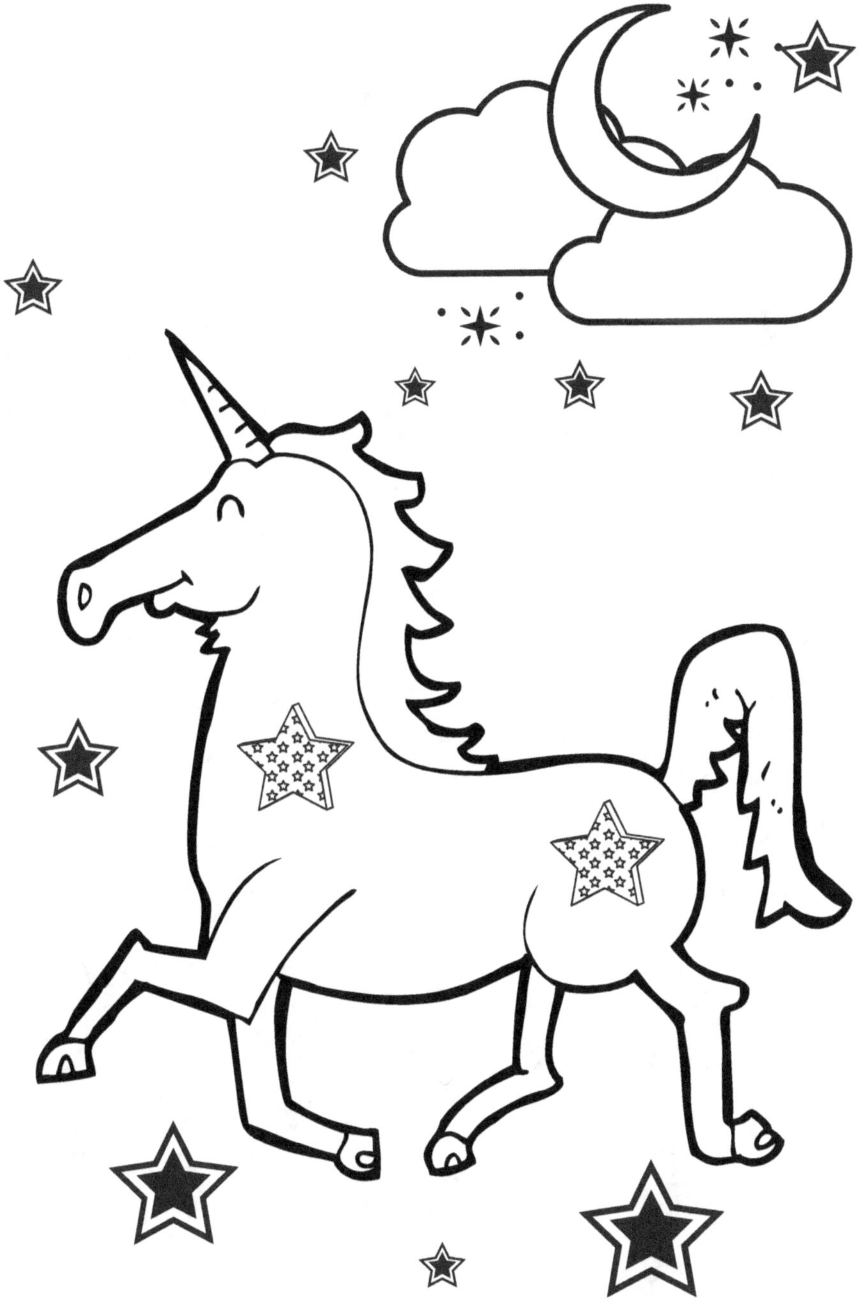

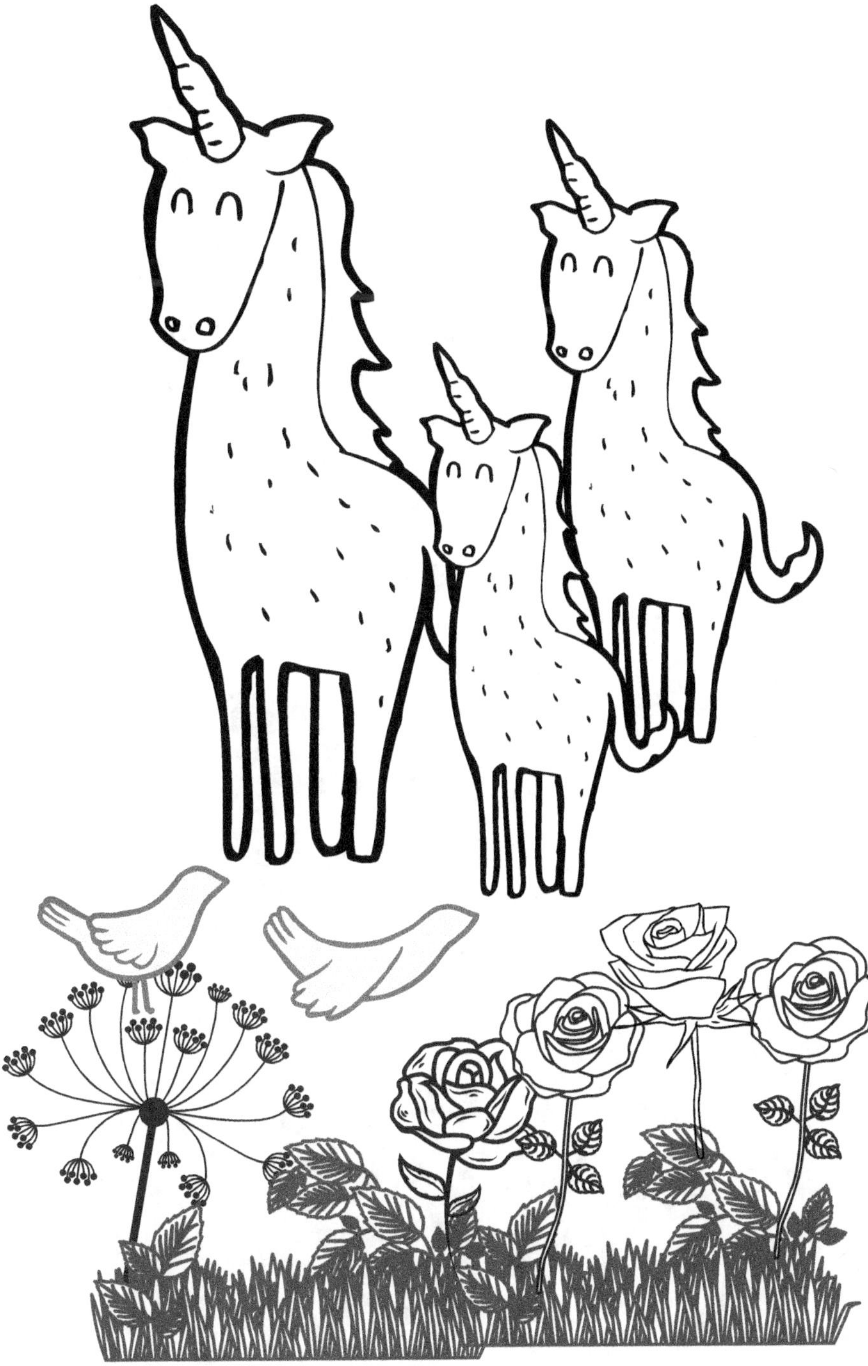

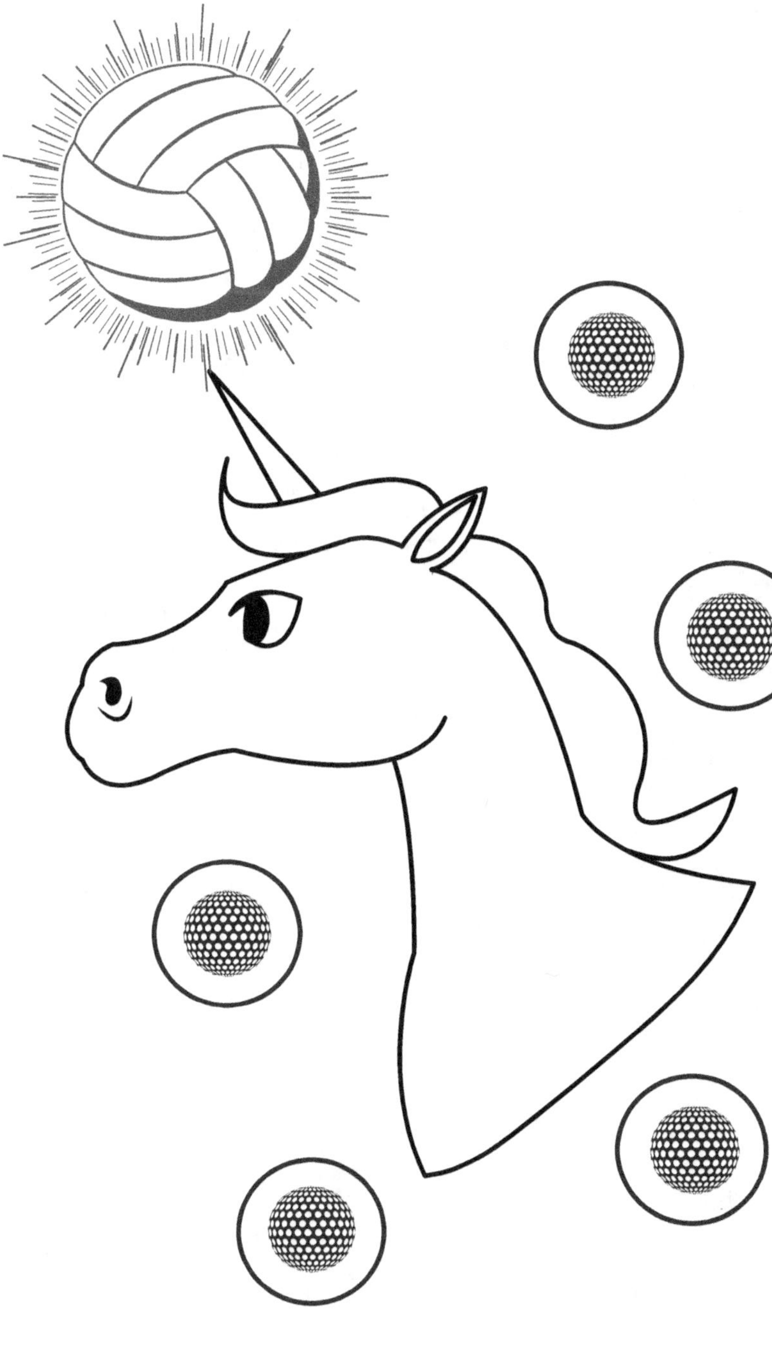

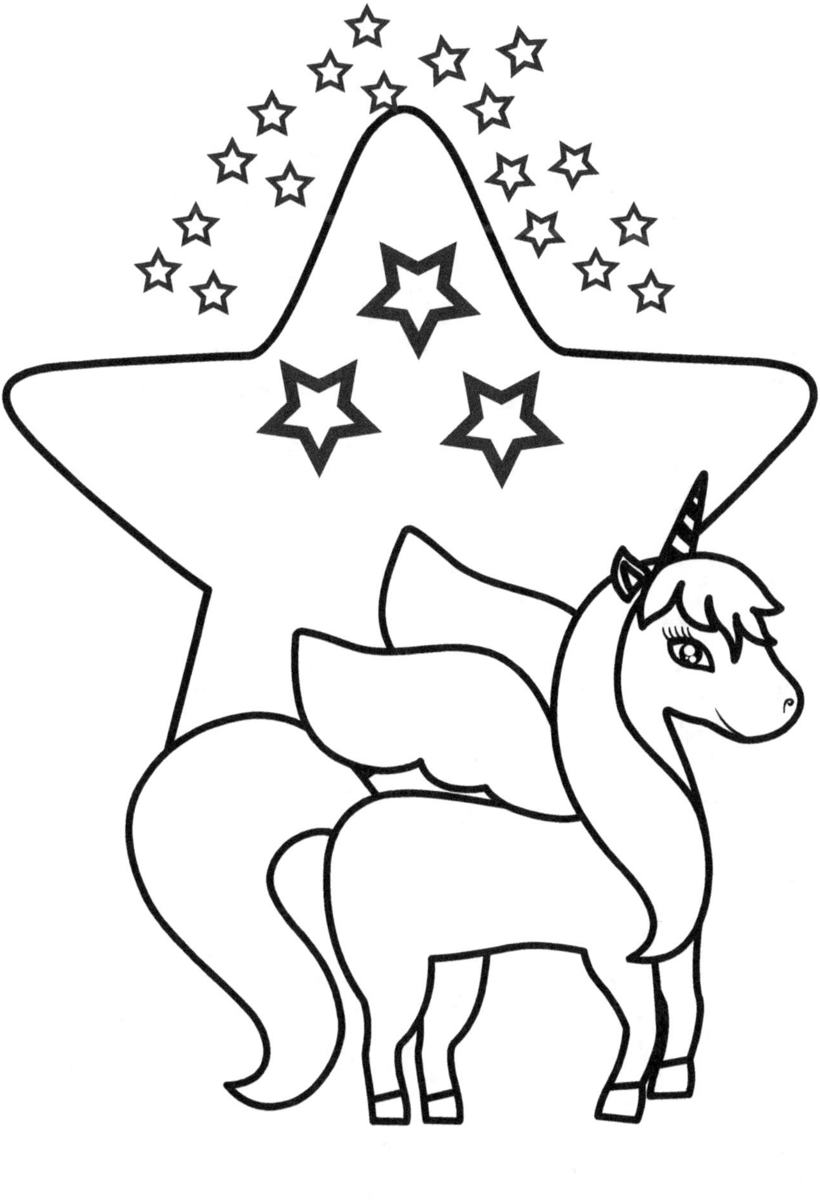

www.ingramcontent.com/pod-product-compliance
Lightning Source LLC
Chambersburg PA
CBHW071124240526
45465CB00023B/816
9798612322474